Snallygaster
The Lost Legend of Frederick County

Patrick Boyton

Copyright © 2008 by Patrick Boyton
All rights reserved. No part of this publication may be reproduced without the prior written permission of the author.

Cover design and illustrations by R.M. Hanson.

ISBN: 978-0-615-25042-7

Visit us on the Web at http://www.marylandmonster.com

To Gram.
For teaching me the value of history.

"In winter's tedious night, sit by the fire, with these old folk, and let them tell thee tales."
             - Madeleine Vinton Dahlgren, *South Mountain Magic*

Table of Contents

Preface 9
Introduction 11
Chapter 1: Beware the Snallygaster! 13
Chapter 2: the Snallygaster Returns 27
Chapter 3: the Beast That Wouldn't Die 35
Chapter 4: the Great Snallygaster Hunt 43
Chapter 5: Origin of the Snallygaster 53
Chapter 6: Sign of the Times 63
Epilogue 67
Bibliography 69
About the Author 73
About the Illustrator 73

Preface

If you are holding this book, perhaps you have an interest in the history of Frederick County. Or maybe you are the type who likes to read spooky folk tales and ghost stories aloud with your friends on a chilly, October night. Whatever your reason for picking up *Snallygaster: the Lost Legend of Frederick County*, my hope is that upon finishing it, you will share the book with a friend and keep the stories contained within these pages alive.

This modest volume is not intended to be an exhaustive cryptozoological study of a mysterious creature. Nor is the book meant to debunk myths or hoaxes surrounding the Snallygaster. My intended goal is to provide a comprehensive history of our local legend. Hopefully, you will enjoy reading about the Snallygaster as much as I've enjoyed researching and writing about it.

This book would not have been possible without the assistance of Mary Mannix, Waneta Gagne, Carolyn Magura, and all of the dedicated volunteers at the C. Burr Artz Public Library's Maryland Room. I would also like to thank the staff of the Middletown Library, as well as the Historical Society of Frederick for their support. Thanks to Patricia Michalak and William Picard for contributing their tremendous editing skills. R.M. Hanson, thank you for the fantastic cover and illustrations. Last but not least, I would like to thank my wife, Melissa, for her continuous love and support.

Now pull up a stump and gather around the campfire (for those at home, a dimly lit lamp will suffice). Let me tell you the tale of the Snallygaster…

Introduction

Along with its natural beauty and rich history, Frederick County is also known for being a hotbed of paranormal activity. Nearly 125 years before amateur ghost hunters flocked to Burkittsville to catch a glimpse of the Blair Witch, local folks told tales of vengeful spirits and mysterious beasts that roamed the region at night.

In 1876, Madeleine Vinton Dahlgren, wealthy widow of Admiral John Dahlgren and a prominent member of Washington's high society, purchased the old South Mountain Inn and turned it into a private summer residence. She became instantly enchanted by her new home just outside Boonsboro, writing an essay entitled "Medievalism in Maryland," where she likened the estate to a medieval castle.

During her tenure at the South Mountain Inn, Mrs. Dahlgren delighted in listening to her neighbors tell of strange legends and superstitions, many of which were of Germanic descent. Mrs. Dahlgren so enjoyed these wild stories of poltergeists and doppelgangers that she collected them in a book, and in 1882, *South Mountain Magic: Tales of Old Maryland* was born.

The stories that make up *South Mountain Magic* are illustrative of a time when South Mountain was a veritable wilderness. After nightfall, the sulfurous fumes of a 20 year old skirmish could still be smelt across the South Mountain Battlefield. On Halloween, mountain mists were said to assume the shapes of men and horses engaged in battle. There are grisly stories of Indian ghosts stalking children, and a woeful tale of a phantom soldier eternally searching the woods for his lost love. A certain woman signaled approaching death to those who saw her pale face in the moonlight.

Strange creatures were seen stalking the countryside, including werewolves, basilisks, banshees and a particularly terrifying demon dog called a "snarly yow." But there was one legend locals feared above all others…

The Snallygaster.

Chapter 1: Beware the Snallygaster!

During the 19th Century, residents of Frederick County, Maryland shared tales of the Snallygaster—a mysterious creature that lives deep in the caves of South Mountain. Stories of a winged beastie that swooped down from the sky to steal chickens and children from unsuspecting town folk had been passed down from generation to generation. Over the course of many years, the legend was woven into the fabric of our region's weird and wonderful folklore.

On February 12, 1909, the Snallygaster leapt from local lore to front page news. As reported in the *Middletown Valley Register*, a man by the name of Bill Gifferson was walking along a country road when a flying monster suddenly dove down upon him. The creature carried its hapless catch to the top of a high hill and proceeded to pierce the victim's jugular vein with its needle-like beak, slowly sucking his blood while gently fanning the man with a set of enormous wings. After finishing its blood feast, the beast tossed Gifferson's drained, lifeless body down the hillside and disappeared into the night sky.

In addition to its wings and beak, the creature was described as having four legs armed with claws like steel hooks and a single eye in the center of its forehead! As if the monster's appearance wasn't terrifying enough, it also emitted a screech that sounded like a locomotive whistle.

As word spread of Gifferson's slaughter, the winged demon was next spotted near Hagerstown. George Jacobs was out hunting when he saw a strange animal with large, flapping wings pass overhead. He thoughtlessly took aim and fired at the creature, but the shot rattled from its tough hide as if he shot against an iron plate. Suddenly the tables were turned and the hunter became the prey! The enraged beast whirled around and chased the terrified gamesman through woods and across a field, its razor-sharp beak snapping hungrily at the nape of the man's neck. Jacobs made a narrow escape by dodging into a stable and slamming the door behind him.

The following night, Mrs. Augustus Ruthrauff of Williamsport was on her way home when she was confronted by the beast. Her characterization of the would-be attacker contradicted that of the previous eyewitnesses. Instead of having talon-like claws, Mrs. Ruthrauff claimed the mystery monster had hoofs. Also, it appeared to have a long, thick tail, like that of a mythical dragon. Despite her paralyzing fear, Mrs. Ruthrauff fled and made it home safely. Whether or not the creature followed the poor woman we'll never know, for she was too afraid to look back. Perhaps its belly was still full from poor ol' Gifferson's vital fluid!

Reports from local papers started flying in that the beast had crossed the Potomac into Shepherdstown, West Virginia. The *Shepherdstown Register* claimed the demon was spotted perched atop the craggy cliffs about a half mile above town. The *Hagerstown Mail* reported that the fiend was seen on the railroad bridge at Shepherdstown the previous Monday night. The engineer of No. 83 described it as having an elastic neck and a very long, sharp beak.

Another eyewitness, whom the *Middletown Valley Register* identifies only as "a gentleman from the southern part of the Valley," claimed that the baddie had laid an egg somewhere in the mountains between Gapland and Burkittsville, although it's exact location was unknown. Reportedly, the egg was nearly as large as a barrel and "covered with a tough, parchment-like shell of yellowish color."

South Mountain postcard

The blood-sucking, winged monster finally gained national attention. According to the *Hagerstown Mail*:

> From descriptions sent to the Smithsonian institute [*sic*] at Washington, they write back that it is either a winged bovulopus or a Snallygaster, as it has some of the characteristics of both. These animals are exceedingly rare and the hide of the Snallygaster is said to be worth a hundred thousand dollars a square foot as it is the only thing known that will properly polish punkle shells used by Africans of Umbopeland for ornaments. Telegrams and letters are pouring in from naturalists, and a strict watch is being kept to try and locate its den or roost.

The word bovulopus has no linguistic history, leaving one to conclude that it was invented by the newspapers' editors in an attempt to give the far-fetched story some "scientific" merit. An additional assumption could be made that the nonsensical word is a combination of *bovine* (of or pertaining to the subfamily Bovinae, which includes cattle, buffalo, and bison) and *lupus* (Latin for wolf). And because the idea of a flying cow-wolf hybrid probably elicited more chuckles than screams, it was Snallygaster that ultimately stuck.

As far as the mysterious African nation of Umbopeland, you're not going to find it on any map, because it doesn't exist and never has. Just as the name bovulopus was used to suggest scientific minds engaged in exciting research, Umbopeland hints of a far off, exotic land filled with strange, undiscovered species. It's important to note that at the beginning of the 20th Century, there still remained unexplored areas in the world's continents. As to what exactly a "punkle shell" looks like, only the good people of Umbopeland know for certain.

On February 11, John T. Baker of Frederick was driving by Lover's Leap, a jagged cliff located at the top of Wills Mountain, overlooking the "Narrows" at Cumberland, Maryland when he saw the Snallygaster flying about 50 feet from the ground. The monster, which the driver described to be about the size of a large horse, nearly frightened the man to death.

The February 12, 1909 edition of the *Middletown Valley Register* followed with a reassuring note: Apparently, the government planned on sending a troop of soldiers armed with a Gaitling gun to kill the feared Snallygaster. Scientists at the Smithsonian Institution wanted to capture it alive, of course. The *Register* added that President Theodore Roosevelt himself was so anxious to see the monster he considered postponing a trip to Africa[1] until its capture.

Furthermore, the *Register* boasted that their "exclusive" Snallygaster story of the week prior created more excitement and

---

[1] In March, 1909, shortly after the end of his second term, President Roosevelt set out for Africa to hunt big game and collect specimens for the Smithsonian Institution. The adventurous ex-president and his 250-member hunting party trekked across British East Africa, into the Belgian Congo, and back to the Nile ending in Khartoum. By the end of their year-long expedition, Roosevelt and his team had collected 1,100 specimens, including 500 big game.

Lover's Leap postcard, circa 1930

discussion in Frederick County than anything since the Spanish-American War. The February 19 front page headline indicated the beast may have come from the West.

THE GREAT GO-DEVIL WAS SEEN IN OHIO

T. C. Harbaugh Saw It Sailing Toward Maryland.

CAME THROUGH CUMBERLAND

Sharpsburgers Building an Incubator to Hatch One of the Big Eggs—Hunting for the Egg Supposed to Be Near Gapland.

According to a letter it received from T.C. Herbage of Casstown, Ohio, dated February 9, 1909:

> A gigantic monster passed over this place last night about 6 o'clock. It was plainly visible, had two immense bronze-like objects as wings, an enormous head from which horns protruded and a tail 20 feet long. It emitted a noise like the screech of an octollopus. Some who saw it declared it to be a Snallygaster. The monster was moving toward Maryland. From the brief view I had of it, I think it was either a octollopus, a gigantiloeutus or a Snallygaster.

The *Cumberland Times* reported that a man working at a brick-burning kiln at Mapleside found an "immense bat" which appeared to be cooling its wings over the outlet of the kiln. When the kiln operator approached the mysterious creature, it let out a yell that could be heard a mile away. The alleged Snallygaster next flapped its wings in anger; the breeze knocked the terrified man over a pile of bricks. The monster then flew over an immense tub of water used to feed the boilers of the brick plant and proceeded to consume its entire contents, nearly one hundred gallons. What happened next is something that has never been reported before or since—the Snallygaster spoke! In a raspy voice, it uttered "My, I'm dry, I haven't had a good drink since I was killed in the battle of Chickamauga."

The Battle of Chickamauga, fought September 18-23, 1863, was the most significant Union defeat in the Western Theater of the Civil War. Western Maryland has always been rich with Civil War ghost stories going back to the earliest days of the conflict between our nation's North and South. What is unusual, however, is this reference to a battle—albeit one of the war's most terrible—that happened some 600 miles away in south-central Tennessee, especially considering Cumberland's close proximity to sites of infamous engagements such as Antietam and Gettysburg. And just what is the lost spirit of a dead soldier doing in the body of a winged "gigantiloeutus" anyway? Since there is no mention of reincarnation in Snally's documented exploits, I think we can safely dismiss the Chickamauga quote as just more editorial mischief-making on the part of the paper's editors.

A gentleman from Hansonville telephoned the *Middletown Valley Register* to say that the Snallygaster had flown over his community about six o'clock that evening. After sucking up and eating all the goldfish from Ramsburg's pond, it flew off with a noise like a mighty "cataraet."[2]

---

[2] The word *cataraet* is most likely an alternate spelling of the word *cataract*, which the *American Heritage Dictionary* defines as "a great waterfall or downpour." To early 20th Century Marylanders, the word may have had a regional significance. On February 8, 1904, according to *The New York Times*, a Baltimore fireboat named The Cataract played a significant part in putting out a fire in that city's waterfront that raged for two days. The *Times* called it "the greatest fire of this generation." While the combined efforts of Washington, Philadelphia, and New York fire

After the winged menace was spotted on Angel Hill and in Scrabble, West Virginia, the *Shepherdstown Register* reported with great excitement that the Snallygaster laid an egg in Alex Crow's barn, located halfway between Shepherdstown and Sharpsburg. Some industrious Sharpsburg men took the egg and actually put it in a large incubator with the intention of hatching it.

Mr. William H. Moore of Yellow Spring, West Virginia phoned the *Middletown Valley Register* to ask for help in securing some Snallygaster eggs for hatching. Allegedly, some bandits had been stealing chickens from Moore's community and he figured that a few young Snallygasters turned loose might put an end to the poultry-snatching. Hadn't Mr. Moore realized that Snally's appetite for fowl was second only to its taste for young children? Recognizing the plan was ill-conceived, the *Register* never followed up on the gentleman's request.

After weeks of reportedly terrorizing communities in Western Maryland and West Virginia's Eastern Panhandle, the Snallygaster appeared to have finally met its match in the form of a brave group of Emmitsburg men. According to the March 5, 1909 edition of the *Emmitsburg Chronicle*, Western Maryland Railway employee Ed Brown was sitting on the bench outside the town's train station, reading a biography of E.H. Harriman[3], while he waited for the evening train. He heard a frightful racket near the coal bunkers. Mr. Brown locked the safe and went out to investigate. Upon counting the coal (coal theft was one of the most common petty larcenies during winter months), Brown knew he had been robbed. "Evidently

---

companies are all credited in helping to extinguish the flames, the "gallant" Cataract was featured as the little engine that turned the tide against the mighty inferno: "The Cataract's was the first victory scored by man in his contest with the fire."

[3] Edward Henry Harriman was a well-known railroad baron who was an important figure of the American railway boom of the late 19th and early 20th Century. At the time of his death in September 1909, Harriman controlled the Union Pacific, the Southern Pacific, the Saint Joseph and Grand Island, the Illinois Central, the Central of Georgia, the Pacific Mail Steamship Company, and the Wells Fargo Express Company.

something is wrong! I can't see the coal," he exclaimed. "Sixteen pieces short!"

EMMITSBURG SAW THE GREAT SNALLYGASTER

It Ate a Coal-Bin Empty and then Spit Fire.

LOOKED LIKE A "COON-SCOOPER"

Its Snout Resembled a Silo and Its Mouth Leaked a Fluid Like Melted Brimstone—Flew Off With a Well.

As Brown was about to track down the coal bandit, the Snallygaster swooped down from above and seized the unsuspecting railway worker by his suspenders! Arriving in the nick of time, local Bill Snider pulled up in his automobile to the sight of Brown dangling in mid-air from the clutches of a winged, one-eyed behemoth. The brave Snider jumped out of his car and dashed to his flailing friend, grabbing him by the foot. After a brief tug-of-war with the devil, Brown's suspenders broke with a snap, sending him crashing to the ground. The creature's "ghost-like" wings beat the air angrily. Suddenly, fire shot from the beast's nostrils, singeing the ground at the feet of the terrified men.

Snider and Brown, with the assistance of local resident Dan Shorb, fought the Snallygaster for nearly an hour and a half before chasing it into the woods of Carroll County. The monster headed for Emmitsburg, where deputy game warden Capt. Norman Hoke showed his badge and, "backed by the full authority of the law," ordered it from the county. Unsurprisingly, Hoke's strong words had little effect on the demon, so local resident Clarence Fraley loaded a gun with croquet balls and slag and shot at it.

The *Middletown Valley Register*'s description of that day's final encounter with the Snallygaster is an especially odd one:

> John Glass, who was returning from a sale at Bridgeport, where he had purchased a well, threw the newly-acquired well at the Sclizthister with such good aim that it is now minus a few ready-made holes, for the well passed over its huge snout and when last seen in the woods to the West of Taneytown it wore it like a nose-ring.

Never mind the *Sclitzhister*! How did Mr. Glass manage to pierce the beasts' snout with a *well*? One can only presume that the story was referring to some sort of ring-like well *part*.

Emmitsburg Train Station, circa 1909 *Photograph courtesy of the*
Emmitsburg Area Historical Society

The notorious showdown with the Snallygaster at the Emmitsburg train station provided *Register* readers with the most terrifying description to date. The mysterious monster's bristly snout was described as resembling a silo, and from the corners of its mouth leaked "a fluid like melted brimstone." Mr. Shorb, who had wrestled with the beast, said its snout looked like a "coon-scooper."[4] Capt. Hoke claimed the devil had a plate brazed on its fin which read "Igonaukus" (a neighboring nation of Umbopeland, perhaps). The most whimsical description of the feared beast goes to Mr. Snider, who described it as looking like "a giraffe on roller-skates."

The decade's last newspaper coverage of the Snallygaster came in the form of a letter to the editor of the *Middletown Valley Register*. The headline, "Origin of the Great Snallygaster," was certainly an eye-grabber, but one would only have to read the opening paragraph to realize that the author's tongue was planted firmly in cheek:

> During the past winter, I read with much interest in the columns of THE VALLEY REGISTER, your very entertaining description of the monster which had made its appearance in the state at that time, and which you were pleased to term as a Snallygaster, Bovapulous, Go-Devil. Believing that many readers of your valuable paper would be pleased to have more definite information relating to the animile (sic), as to its origin, size, appearance, etc., with your kind permission, I will gladly endeavor to supply the same, said information having been recently obtained from one of a number of eminent scientists sent out by the Department of "Gyascutimoses," or in other words, the "Department of Mental Gymnastics."

The author went on to claim that the Snallygaster is part of an ancient species that originates from the bowels of the earth and is liberated only by an earthquake. The creature in question was actually

---

[4] The term *coon-scooper* is most likely another word for *cow catcher*: A V-shaped wedge attached to the front of a train in order to clear obstacles off the track.

released, the letter went on to say, as the result of a recent earthquake in Italy.⁵ Shortly thereafter, the beast was spotted on South Mountain, east of Crothersville and near Burkittsville.

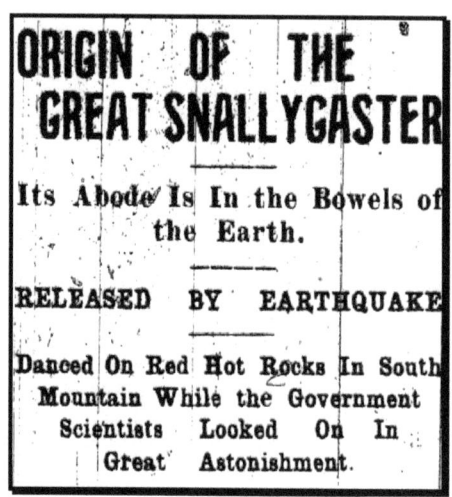

According to the author, the aforementioned Department's agents were dispatched at once. The scientists made many visits to the mountain, but evidence of "his satanic majesty" could not be found. Just as they had reached the conclusion that further research on their part would be in vain, something caught their attention at the midnight hour: a brilliant, bright light on the summit of South Mountain. The intrepid agents followed the mysterious light to the mountain's peak, and there discovered what they had been searching for —the lair of the beast!

As the team approached the mouth of a cave, a strange noise emitted from within, described as being similar to that produced by a

---

⁵ On December 28, 1908, the Sicilian city of Messina was devastated by an earthquake and associated tsunami that left 60,000 dead and destroyed most of the ancient architecture. The catastrophe is considered to be one of the worst natural disasters in recorded history to date.

"steam calliope[6], or the wailing of lost souls." Following in the direction of the noise, the scientists were suddenly greeted with flashes of flames, which spurted to a great height from a fissure in the mountain. As day began to dawn, the flashes of flames died away, the strange noise ceased, and the fissure closed up completely, leaving no traces of its existence.

Concluding that the creature's activity was nocturnal, the team of scientists returned to the mountain's peak the following evening. As dusk blanketed South Mountain, the brave agents waited patiently. Before long, the ground rumbled and the earth split open, spitting flames high into the night sky. Out of the fire emerged the Snallygaster like a mighty phoenix. It was described as "a cross between a jackass, a hyena, a baboon and the devil, having a forked tail, immense horns, cloven hoofs, fiery eyes and a screech like a steam siren and in size equaling an elephant." After exhibiting itself in the flames for over an hour, the devil sailed up to a great height and then flew in a westerly direction toward Shepherdstown. The scientists watched in awe as the monster flew over the Potomac River, its giant wings glinting in the moonlight. After bathing itself in the river, the creature disappeared into a cave on the Virginia shore.

As day broke, the monster returned to its lair in the mountain, "its horns gory with blood, evidencing the fact that it had secured another victim." As before, the rumbling noise suddenly ceased, the flames died away, and the fissure closed up.

The Snallygaster wasn't seen or heard from again for another 23 years.

---

[6] Also known as a "steam organ" or "steam piano", a calliope was a steam-whistle musical organ used to attract attention for circuses and fairs at the turn of the 20th Century. Its loud, shrill sound could be heard for miles.

Chapter 2: the Snallygaster Returns

By 1932, the once dreaded Snallygaster had become a distant memory to the people of Western Maryland. Nearly a quarter century had passed without a sign of the beast. No sightings. No footsteps. The legend was relegated to the status it held before the winter of 1909—that of a quaint, local folktale. The winged monster that had made headlines and kept families locked in their homes at night was now merely a cautionary tale told to children: *"Better get to sleep or the Snallygaster will get ya!"* But as the children slept, something deep inside South Mountain waited patiently to resurrect its reign of terror.

Forgotten fears were reignited in the hearts of local residents when they opened the *Middletown Valley Register* on the morning of November 11, 1932, to the following headline:

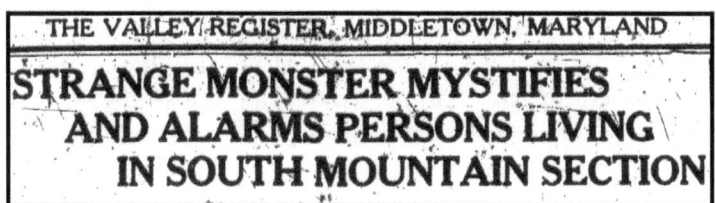

Citing an article published in the *Boonsboro Times* the previous week, the *Register* reported that a number of people living in

South Mountain—particularly those residing in Clevelandville and Appletown—claimed to have seen a strange monster flying over the region. The descriptions of the beast were even more outrageous than those reported in 1909. According to eyewitnesses, the Snallygaster would "change color and size and at times throw out long streamers like the arms of an octopus, only to draw them in again and sail out of sight." As the monster appeared to be flying overhead, residents sought safety within their homes. The winged beastie kept its distance, appearing and disappearing behind the mountain, making no effort to harm anyone.

Speculation ran high that this was the very same Snallygaster that terrorized Frederick and Washington Counties in 1909. This theory was quickly deemed unlikely by "scientists" who claimed that the average lifespan of a "Bovulopus" to be only 25 years. A *Register* reporter, who visited some of the South Mountain locations where the monster was seen, speculated that it was probably hatched from one of the eggs laid by the Snallygaster 23 years ago. The scientists went on to claim that "it takes 20 to 25 years for one of these eggs to hatch, and if such is the case, this could easily be an offspring of the 'Go-Devil' which was seen in this section in 1909." The article concluded with a plea to eyewitnesses to come forward with their descriptions in view of the monster's "scientific value."

Within weeks, reports of the mysterious creature were pouring in. The November 25, 1932 edition of the *Middletown Valley Register* covered a sighting by two local residents:

> While returning home from Frederick early Tuesday morning, Charles F. Main, Middletown ice cream manufacturer, and Edward M.L. Lighter, were frightened nearly out of their wits when the beast suddenly appeared flying over the National highway towards Catoctin Mountain, near the old "white house", just east of Braddock Heights. Both state that the "Snallygaster" appeared suddenly from the south and was flying not more than 25 feet in the air, which afforded them an excellent view of the monster.

For a moment, the men stated, it appeared as if the strange beast was headed directly toward their automobile, but it suddenly headed north towards the mountain when it was only about 50 feet from them. In accordance with the paper's recent descriptions, Mr. Main said that the creature changed color several times, at first appearing white and then black. The monster's wingspan appeared to be between 12 and 14 feet. After waiting some time, the gentlemen finally mustered up enough nerve to investigate the area on the mountain where they thought the beast landed. When they arrived there, however, all traces of the monster had disappeared.

> **2 Middletown Men See "Snallygaster" Tuesday Morning**
>
> Chas. F. Main and Edward M. L. Lighter Frightened By the Strange Beast, Near Braddock Heights.

On another occasion, a pair of young boys, Junior Fulmer and "Buddy" Haupt, reported seeing a strange monster flying towards Middletown from South Mountain. Needless to say, the boys didn't wait long enough to see in which direction the beast went, and instead "scurried to their homes as fast as their legs could take them."

While the newspaper reports prompted some local residents to lock their doors at night, others were more amused by the Snallygaster's sudden return. Mrs. Lewis E. Jones expressed her delight in a letter to the *Middletown Valley Register*'s editor on November 28, 1932:

Dear Sir –

This wonderful story of the "Snallygaster", which is being printed in "The Register", is truly interesting, I assure you, and looking at it from all angles, we find it very humorous as well. Should this monster ever be captured, we hope that you will print its picture in "The Register". I derive a lot of pleasure in clipping the news from the paper and sending it on to my friends, instead of condemning our good editor for publishing the story in "The Register". Come on, Charles F. Main and Edward M.L. Lighter, and give us more about the monster. I, for one subscriber, enjoy reading it.

As the story of the Snallygaster's return gained momentum, elder residents began to speak of a "Jabberwock"[7] that terrorized Frederick more than 50 years before. According to the December 1, 1932 edition of the *Frederick Post*, one of the city's "best known residents" recalled a panic similar to the one caused by the recent Snallygaster sighting. For a long time, tales were told concerning a horrible face that would peer into the windows of homes along McMurray Street. The creature was often seen scaling the street's high fences while "persons residing in the houses watched spellbound." Children screamed upon hearing mention of the Jabberwock and were forbidden to be outside after sunset by their equally frightened parents. For months the terror continued to plague the people of Frederick. Everyone was on the lookout for the "monster of monsters."

On December 12, 1932 the Snallygaster enjoyed a brief bit of national attention over the airwaves, as reported in the *Frederick News*:

---

[7] The name of in the poem "Jabberwocky" was the name of Lewis Carroll's monster in his novel *Through the Looking Glass, and What Alice Found There* (1871).

Over a coast-to-coast radio hook-up came details of the weird monster of Middletown Valley, supplied by Lowell Thomas[8] in his regular news talk at 6:45 o'clock from New York city. Mr. Thomas devoted about five or six minutes of his 15 minute news summary to a description of the antics of the strange creature, which was the talk of the county just a week or so ago.

Thousands of radio listeners from Boston to Seattle heard how the Snallygaster supposedly swooped into Middletown Valley, frightening several people nearly out of their wits. Mr. Thomas quoted from the story as it appeared in the *News* and referred to other newspapers that carried the strange tale.

Local residents breathed a collective sigh of relief as they read the *Middletown Valley Register* on the morning of December 12. The front page headline announced the death of the Snallygaster! Allegedly, the Bovulopus was attracted to the Frog Hollow section of Washington County by fumes arising from a 2,500 gallon vat of moonshine. Just as the beast flew over the vat it was overcome by the fumes and fell directly into the steaming hot mash, becoming submerged completely. The five moonshiners attending to the illicit still fled the state before they could witness the monster's demise.

George T. Danforth, in charge of the Hagerstown prohibition office, accompanied by Agent Charles E. Cushwa, arrived at the scene after receiving a tip about the moonshine plant only to find it abandoned. As they approached the still bubbling vat, the men made a grisly discovery. The mash had eaten away all of the monster's skin, leaving behind only the skeletal remains of the once mighty

---

[8] Lowell Jackson Thomas was an American writer, broadcaster, and traveler best known as the man who made T.E. Lawrence famous. Thomas shot dramatic footage of Lawrence during World War I that he made into a highly successful documentary entitled W*ith Allenby in Palestine and Lawrence in Arabia.* Thomas was fictionalized in David Lean's film *Lawrence of Arabia* as American journalist Jackson Bentley, played by Arthur Kennedy.

Snallygaster. This rapid corrosion was attributed to the large amount of lye[9] which had been placed in the mash.

Mr. Danforth and Mr. Cushwa, determined to obliterate the beast once and for all, secured 500 pounds of dynamite under the vat and lit the fuse, "thus ending the career of the 'Go-Devil' for all time to come."

Or so they believed.

---

[9] In the past, moonshine was often mixed with lye to fool people into believing it was of a higher proof.

Middletown Valley Register, December 12, 1932

Chapter 3: the Beast That Wouldn't Die

Like any good news story, the tale of the Snallygaster refused to go away. Less than two years after allegedly meeting its end in a vat of illicit liquor, news of the return of the resilient beast splashed across the front page of the *Frederick News* on July 23, 1934:

"*SNALLYGASTER STORY IS REVIVED IN MIDDLETOWN*"

Edward Lewis, a resident of the Pleasant Walk section of Middletown Valley, was keeping watch of his farm after some of his chickens had disappeared the week before. The farmer suspected that the poultry thief was perhaps the "large, strange bird" that locals had recently reported seeing coming down from the mountain. Mr. Lewis's suspicions were validated when he encountered a strange creature that he described as being four and one-half feet tall, with a wingspan of six feet. Its bill was four inches long, as were its claws. Not taking any chances, Lewis shot the beast. Although badly wounded, the monster made an attempt to attack one of the farmer's children. In order to protect his kin from the clutches of the beast, Lewis fired a second shot. As quickly as the Snallygaster had returned to resurrect its reign of terror, it was gone again.

Due to its relatively small size, authorities speculated that this latest Snallygaster was a "baby". The offspring was believed to have hatched from one of several eggs laid by its mother before she was killed in a vat of moonshine in 1932. As for the "scientific" theory that it takes 20 to 25 years for a Snallygaster egg to hatch, the *Post* offered a convenient explanation: the exceptionally warm weather[10] that summer caused the eggs to hatch about 20 years ahead of schedule.

In the summer of 1947, local interest in the Snallygaster revived as paranoid citizens watched the skies for a new kind of menace—flying saucers. The July 8, 1947 edition of the *Frederick News* fueled the UFO fever that was sweeping the nation with the following article reporting an area sighting:

> The theory that objects might be "flying saucers" was flouted in many quarters. Bruce T. O'Hara, 423 South Market Street, was sketching in his backyard when the dots appeared in the sky, approaching fast out of the north and traveling in the general direction of Washington. His attention first attracted by the odd sound, Mr. O'Hara glanced up to see what he thought to be jet planes. "There were five of them and they were in formation," he said. "I never seen anything like them before." R. O'Hara ran into the house to tell his family but by the time they reached the yard, the objects had vanished from the sky. His interest captured by the flying objects, Mr. O'Hara communicated with the *Post*. He had no idea they were "flying saucers," he said, but wondered if they might be associated with the recent phenomenon[11] that had attracted so much national attention.

---

[10] According to the National Weather Bureau, 1934 "was abnormally warm nearly everywhere; only small areas in Michigan and North Carolina, and portions of New Jersey, New York and New England averaged cooler than normal."

[11] On July 7, 1947 the United States military recovered strange materials near Roswell, New Mexico. While the military maintained what they recovered was a top-secret research balloon, many UFO theorists believe the wreckage was of a crashed alien spacecraft. The "Roswell Incident" continues to be the subject of great debate, speculation and doubt among conspiracy theorists and UFOologists.

The *News* was quick to ride the flying saucer wave to promote its own front porch legend. "Flying saucers? They cause little reaction in Middletown valley," the paper scoffed. "Middletowners have had snallygasters to talk about since 1909." After recapping the monster's recorded exploits of 1909 and 1932, the writer ended the article with an ominous cliff-hanger: "There is a rumor that the snallygaster left some eggs which are just about ready to hatch."

In a *Baltimore Evening Sun* letter to the editor dated September 7, 1951, Charles F. Stein went so far as to propose that the Snallygaster and flying saucer were actually one and the same. Mr. Stein claimed that "an alleged 'Flying Saucer' seen over Hagerstown[12] was subsequently identified by an astronomer as being a large snallygaster."

An unnamed Middletown Valley farmer came face to face with the dreaded dragon *four* times, according to Mr. Stein. The anonymous farmer had three brushes with the beast while hunting on South Mountain, and once when it raided his barn. The farmer friend told Mr. Stein that the best protection against the Snallygaster's raids is to paint a seven pointed star on the barn. But he cautioned, "The star must be drawn very accurately, or it will not be effective."

Just as reports of the Snallygaster began to die down, the July 12, 1952 edition of *The Washington Post* posed a provocative question: "Is it really alive, or does Western Maryland's famed 'snallygaster' have a twin?"

According to the article, during the past two years, there had been persistent reports that a big black bear was ranging in Frederick

---

[12] According to case 413 in Ted Bloecher's *Report on the UFO Wave of 1947*, on July 6, 1947, Mrs. Madelyn Ganoe of 349 South Cannon Avenue, Hagerstown, "saw a group of five 'saucer-shaped' objects flying at 'terrific speed' through cloudy skies." She described the flat objects as having "something on the back end" like a fin. Mrs. Ganoe said the objects emitted a sound "the likes of which I have never heard before." She described it as "like the roar of a far away train," but was otherwise unable to compare it with anything familiar. She said the objects were quickly lost to view when they disappeared behind trees.

and Washington Counties. "Skeptics say the animal is a cousin or twin to the legendary snallygaster." Those who claimed to have seen tracks in a Hagerstown park said that they were too big to belong to a domestic animal and were clearly the print of a paw, not a hoof. Park caretakers could not recall any unusual pets in the neighborhood, but one man said he saw a "strange-looking animal lumbering around the edge of the park at night."

On August 28, 1953, *The Washington Post* once again invoked our winged celebrity with the announcement of yet another creature terrorizing Maryland:

> **Said Witness: 'If You Want It Watched, Watch It Yourself'**
> **Gorilla-Like Beast Seen Roaming Woods Near Elkton—In Md.'s 'Snallygaster' Country**

According to the article, there was a "definite possibility" that a large gorilla-like animal was loose in the heavily wooded area along the Maryland-Pennsylvania line in Cecil County.

Farmers H.S. Osborne and Ray Potter claimed to have seen the strange creature from about 20 feet away. Osborne said it was about three o'clock in the afternoon, the light was good, and when he and Potter looked toward the woods, the animal was peering over the fence at them. Osborne described it as "about six feet tall, brownish hair all over and a pink ring around its face." The creature stood erect and had a monkey-like appearance. Osborne told Potter to keep an eye on the creature while he ran inside to fetch his shotgun. When he got to the door and looked back, Potter was right behind him.

"If you want it watched, watch it yourself," a clearly shaken Potter told his friend. When they returned, the mystery monster was gone.

Joseph Eggers, who spotted the beast as it disappeared into a corn field, described it as being brownish and about the size of a man. Game warden Monroe C. Peeden, Jr. corroborated Eggers's account when he found 20 ears of corn scattered around a clearing in the woods. The husks had been pulled back on most of the ears and several rows of corn had been eaten. Fred Ulmer, curator of mammals at the Philadelphia Zoo, ruled out the possibility that the animal was a gorilla "both because of their scarcity and their high value."

Like the Snallygaster before it, this new gorilla-like menace was keeping fearful residents locked up in their homes at night. Farmers kept their firearms handy and warned that "if it was somebody dressed in a monkey suit, he was monkeying with death because they were going to shoot on sight." This article is particularly noteworthy because it contains the first reference to the Snallygaster inhabiting Eastern Maryland: "This area is near the haunt of the mythical snallygaster, a flying sea monster[13] said alternately to inhabit the Chesapeake Bay and the Middletown Valley west of here."

Over a decade passed without a glimpse of the Snallygaster. The year was 1965 and Western Maryland appeared to have finally rid itself of the Go-Devil and its alleged bear/gorilla brethren. But just when locals thought it was safe to go camping up in South Mountain, Ol' Snally came back. And this time, he was going by a new name.

The Dwayyo.

Frederick News staff writer George May ran a series of articles during November and December about a hairy, black biped that was supposedly terrorizing Frederick County. Timothy L. Cannon and Nancy F. Whitmore described one such encounter in their 1979 book, *Ghosts and Legends of Frederick County*:

> On Saturday evening, November 27, 1965, near the woods of Gambrill State Park, "John Becker" went out in his yard to investigate a strange noise. It was getting dark, and he had started back to the house, when he saw it – something moving toward him. "It was as big as a bear, had long black hair, a bushy tail, and

---

[13] This appears to be the only occasion where the Snallygaster is referred to as a "sea monster." Perhaps the author confused it with Chessie, a legendary sea serpent said to live in the Chesapeake Bay.

growled like a wolf or a dog in anger." As it got closer, it stood up on its hind legs and attacked him. "Becker" fought the creature until it ran into the woods, leaving him, his wife and children in horror. Deciding to remain anonymous under the alias John Becker, he filed a report with local police, telling of an attack by a mysterious monster called a *Dwayyo*.[14]

Soon newspapers throughout the area were carrying the story. And because the Dwayyo (pronounced Dway-yo with accent on the first syllable) had been seen around the Snallygaster's old stomping ground, it wasn't long before May linked the two local legends in the March 3, 1965 edition of the *Frederick News Post*:

> **You'd Better Watch Out**
> **'Dwayyo' Could Be A Modern Snallygaster**

A Burkittsville resident, who reminded readers that the Snallygaster's eggs hatch every 20 years, speculated that the Snallygaster and the Dwayyo could be connected by birth. "The eggs should be hatching just about now," he said. "The Dwayyo could actually be a Snallygaster."

The following description closed the chapter on the incarnation of the Snallygaster Marylanders had come to know and

---

[14] While "John Becker" is often credited for coining the name "Dwayyo," the moniker was actually used to describe a similar creature spotted around Gambrill State Park in the 1920s, according to Janet and Colin Bord's *Bigfoot Casebook*.

fear for generations—that of a one-eyed, winged dragon with tentacles and a needle-like bill:

> So old Snallygaster, move over. A challenger has arisen to attempt a takeover as the most mysterious creature ever to roam Frederick County. The challenger, of course, is the tall, black mysterious Dwayyo which is being seen and heard throughout the county. The Dwayyo could become this area's most famous monster.
>
> The Snallygaster had evolved.

Chapter 4: the Great Snallygaster Hunt

The Washington Post, perhaps emboldened by their recent Watergate exposé and Richard Nixon's subsequent resignation, decided to take on Maryland's most famous legend in the fall of 1976. Staff writer Gordon Chaplin's report, titled "The Grand Bicentennial Washington Post/Potomac Expedition to Darkest Maryland in Search of the Monstrous Snallygaster," was a colorful chronicle of his attempts to capture the dreaded beast in the White Marsh area of Anne Arundel County. Published in the Sunday edition of the *Post* on October 10, Chaplin's article was a delightfully irreverent piece of gonzo journalism.

Taking a page from George May, Chaplin notes the Dwayyo's influence on the Snallygaster's appearance over the previous 11 years:

> It is described both in Webster's Third International Dictionary and the 1935 Federal Writer's Project Guide as part reptile, part bird, but those who claim to have seen it recently say it more closely resembles the Sasquatch or Bigfoot of the Northwestern rainforests. Like the Bigfoot, the Snallygaster is said to be ape-like, much bigger than a man, and covered with shaggy hair.

With his reference to "Sasquatch," Chaplin was clearly trying to capitalize on the Bigfoot craze of the 1970s.[15]

To prepare for his monster quest, Chaplin called upon the services of Cruttwell's of London:

> General James H.G. Cruttwell, F.R.G.S., runs an expedition outfitting house in London and has himself been an imposing figure, as novelist Evelyn Waugh[16] wrote. Cruttwell's Glacier in Spitzbergen, Cruttwell Falls in Venezuela, Mount Cruttwell in the Pamirs, Cruttwell's Leap in Cumberland mark his travels.

Chaplin wrote, "Cruttwell's was one of few places in the world that could outfit our trip in the style it deserved."

An expedition of this magnitude required an incredible range of equipment, and the *Post* spared no expense. The gear needed to be light and easily portable but strong enough to weather the area's strong storms. While the author admitted that killing the animal would lead to inevitable preservation league accusations, he still demanded weaponry to defend his party in the event of an attack. Extensive medical supplies were ordered in case of injury, as was extra-sensitive optical equipment to photograph the elusive creature. For cooking, they brought an authentic "Roosevelt Pressure Cooker."[17] Other

---

[15] Bigfoot maintained a high profile in popular culture throughout the decade, thanks to "Sasquatchploitation" movies such as *The Legend of Boggy Creek* (1972) and *Legend of Bigfoot* (1975).

[16] Clearly intended to be an inside joke aimed at literary types, this passage is lifted verbatim from Waugh's *Scoop* (1938), a satire of sensational journalism. In several of his novels, Waugh named his most loathsome characters "Cruttwell," out of an enduring hatred of his former college dean, CRMF Cruttwell. In the 1920s at Hertford College, Oxford, one of Dean Cruttwell's lectures was heckled by a drunken undergraduate student by the name of Evelyn Waugh. Cruttwell called Waugh "a silly little suburban sod with an inferiority complex and no palate - Drinks Pernod after meals!" Waugh infamously retaliated against the insult by circulating a rumor that Cruttwell liked to sodomize dogs.

eclectic items on the expedition checklist included a bible, humidor, astrolabe[18], Moet© champagne, ten pounds of Beluga caviar, and a custom crafted flagstaff emblazoned with the *Washington Post* logo.

After news of the expedition began to filter through the Washington D.C. Metro Area, the *Post* received requests from hundreds of people eager to join the adventure. "Ranging from bartenders and taxi drivers to atomic scientists, diplomats, even some politicians, they all wanted to catch a glimpse of the monster." But in an effort to streamline the hunting party, Chaplin quoted historical Snallygaster enthusiast Teddy Roosevelt: "In a country where every additional ounce of baggage counts against you, it is necessary to cut all personnel to the bone."

Chaplin boiled the expedition down to five of the most qualified people in Washington and "perhaps the country":

> Dick Swanson, for six years a *Life* Magazine photographer in Vietnam, would be expedition photographer in charge of defense and

---

[17] As the United States entered World War II, the conversion of farmers into soldiers and the rationing of gasoline were putting a strain on both food supplies and our ability to transport fruits and vegetables to market. Claude Wickard, the Secretary of Agriculture, tried to put a stop to a grass roots home gardening movement that had begun to take root across the country. Wickard believed in a top down, industrial approach to food production, and felt that home gardens would be an inadequate solution to feed the country and our war machine. Eleanor Roosevelt, however, firmly believing that massive amounts of food production could quickly and efficiently be de-centralized, planted a "victory garden" on the lawn of the White House. Under the formidable political pressure of this extraordinary woman, Wickard relented and 20 million "victory gardens" were planted and nurtured by 50 million inexperienced, first time farmers. These men and women went on to produce 9 to 10 million tons of fresh fruit and vegetables, providing nearly 50 % of the nation's needs. Pressure cooker sales would grow from 66,000 in 1942 to 315,000 in 1943 as a new nation of urban and suburban "food producers" began canning their own fruits and vegetables.

[18] An *astrolabe* is an ancient astronomical instrument used by classical astronomers, astrologers, and navigators to locate and predict the positions of the sun, moon, planets and stars.

pharmaceuticals. Brian and Danuta Lockett, the first husband-and-wife team to live successfully for an extended period of time in the Big Thicket of Texas, would handle expedition logistics and organization. Ginny Durrin, the documentary filmmaker now working with Margo St. James on a cinematic study of prostitution, would oversee sound, lighting and special effects. My wife Helen, who has studied homeopathic medicine and spiritual astrology under Isabel Hickey in Boston, agreed to act as expedition psychic and healer.

Swanson was the only party member Chaplin had any reservations about. A close friend, the author described the photographer as being unpredictable and moody, "liable even to turn violent under the worst circumstances." But due to Swanson's brilliant eye, Chaplin decided that having him along was well worth the risk. Besides, with his extensive battlefield experience, the veteran "could be counted on to keep a cool head in the most bizarre situations."

Distancing himself from the tabloid sensationalism favored by his journalist predecessors, Chaplin approached the Snallygaster from a decidedly more cryptozoological[19] perspective. To back up his belief that such a creature may actually walk among us, the author brought up two examples popular within crypto communities: The gorilla and the coelacanth.

When French-American explorer Paul de Chaillu returned from a trip to the Congo in 1856 and described his encounter there with a hairy giant that stood "nearly six feet high, with an immense body, huge chest and muscular arms," scientists laughed at him. We now know that du Chaillu was the first white man to see a gorilla. "Gorillas did not exist in 1856," Chaplin argued, "simply because the desk-bound scientists of London and Paris said they did not exist. Snallygasters do not officially exist in 1976 for precisely the same reason."

---

[19] *Cryptozoology* is the study of and search for animals that fall outside of contemporary zoological categories.

To strengthen his argument, Chaplin reminded readers of what biologist Ivan T. Sanderson wrote[20] about the discovery of the coelacanth fish:

> "On the hearing of the initial announcement of such a fishy thing having been obtained by a Dr. Latimer of the Port Elizabeth Museum in South Africa, a Doctor of Piscology, i.e. Ichthyology, stated the record that it was impossible because 'we all know' that all coelacanths have been totally extinct for some 70 million years. That was August 1938. In August 1948, the same great expert stated: "This is probably the greatest zoological discovery of all time."

Chaplin often displayed an almost Ahab-like obsession with tracking down the elusive monster: "Personally, I'd always wanted to believe in the Snallygaster. Sometimes I've wanted desperately to believe in it." If seeing was believing, Chaplin was looking forward to becoming a Snallygaster disciple.

As soon as the expedition was secure, Chaplin visited the Baltimore home of Snallygaster expert, John Lutz[21], to gather pertinent information. Lutz, who had been investigating unidentified flying objects and other unexplained phenomena in Maryland since 1962, knew a thing or two about Snallygaster expeditions. Lutz had led a giant search party up the Patapsco River in search of the Bigfoot-like creature in 1972. Although Lutz came short of seeing the mysterious creature, the 1972 hunt produced the only known piece of

---

[20] Although no credit is provided, Ivan T. Sanderson's quote appears to have been lifted from John A. Keel's crypto-classic, *Strange Creatures From Time and Space* (1970).

[21] As John Lutz stated in a *Citypaper* interview from March 23, 2005, "We investigated every type of strange phenomenon there was. I was the only independent researcher in the United States that had a statewide police agency calling me, saying, 'Well, we got a mysterious animal on the Beltway,' or, 'There's a mysterious light on Route 24 outside of Rocks State Park.'"

physical evidence related to the beast: a pair of plaster casts made from 13-inch long, three-toed feet.

Lutz had been involved in investigating a recent rash of sightings in the swamps around Bird River northeast of Baltimore. Richard and Elva Stewart had been clearing brush near the edge of a grove of trees when they heard branches breaking and smelled an odor like swamp water. "It kept coming so we ran for the house," Mrs. Stewart said. "I looked back and saw something about eight feet tall with two big, red eyes." A few nights later, the Stewarts heard scratching noise outside of the house. The next morning, they found scratch marks on the outside of the house at a height of nine feet.

According to the county police, the Stewarts were not the only residents in the area to see the behemoth biped. One woman reported a grassy area where the beast apparently had slept. Neighbors spoke of large, mysterious footprints and disrupted vegetable gardens. Lutz told Chaplin that there had been other sightings in the Bird River area but "we have tried to keep them out of the paper because things down there were getting out of hand. People are getting panicky, walking around with guns. One girl almost killed 6 people with a .38 pistol."

Lutz went on to speculate that the Snallygaster might have an "extra dimension:"

> He had heard of a law enforcement officer in Pennsylvania who fired at it 6 times with a .357 Magnum only to have it disappear in a soundless flash of light. Another time, he said, two policemen spotted it walking in a field. As their line of vision on it changed, it became invisible *to one of them.*

"I'm not fully convinced these things have a physical existence as we understand it," Lutz said. "We may be dealing with something from a time warp." And in an eerie parallel with Charles F. Stein's 1951 letter to *The Baltimore Evening Sun,* Lutz said, "You know, it's very strange, but people smell the same smell when there are UFOs around." Taking another quote from Keel's book, Chaplin concurred that the region was a "typical window area, marked by continuous

UFO activity, bizarre monster sightings, and the mysterious comings and goings of unusual persons."

In addition to speculating that the Snallygaster might have had extraterrestrial origins, Lutz also suggested that the monster may be psychic. "I think these things can read your thoughts," he said. "You can be in the right place at the right time, but you'll never see it unless you are *thinking* right."

Helen Chaplin awoke from an ominous dream the morning of their departure. In the dream, she had been in a dark forest "brilliantly lit from the inside." Someone or something had been singing and calling her name in between verses. "The animal's waiting for us," she told her husband. Chaplin described that morning with a great sense of foreboding. A thick ground mist had been left by pre-dawn rain and he saw odd "omens" everywhere: A crushed dog on the road outside their house, thousands of slugs climbing their terrace walls, and garbage strewn about on the neighbor's lawn.

The crate of supplies from Cruttwell's arrived at the Port of Baltimore via the *Kora Sea*. When the party arrived to load up their equipment, they found it was being held by U.S. Customs, due to the caviar, which was fresh, not canned. Apparently, the Customs Officers could not pass the Beluga because the eggs might hatch, potentially wreaking the Chesapeake oyster harvest. Concerned that the caviar might have contaminated the entire shipment, Customs insisted upon spraying the crate contents with DDT and quarantining them for six months. Suspiciously eyeing the giant red crate embossed with the Cruttwell's logo, one of the officers sniffed, "I wouldn't let them in even without the eggs." At last, a discreet call was made to "higher authorities" and it was agreed that the other supplies could be released if they left the Beluga behind.

Tom Sobotka, a White Marsh crabber, was hired to guide the party up Bird River. Described as "small and wiry," Sobotka used diving skills he learned as a Navy Underground Demolition in Vietnam to explore the Chesapeake. Having spent "Ninety percent of his time in his small crabbing boat, underwater, or in the swamps," Sobotka knew the area's swampland better than anyone else. And he claimed to know where the Snallygaster dwelled, in a high piece of ground in the center of Stump's Swamp.

Stump's Swamp, where it was said "a man who stepped in the wrong place could sink over his head in a matter of seconds," was a place where no Snallygaster hunter, including Lutz, had ever ventured. "There are tunnels that start way down deep in the bay and come up in the middle of the swamp," Sobotka explained. "There are things out on the islands off Edgewood that nobody would believe. Nobody goes out there but me. If I told you everything I saw up there they'd lock me up."

Due to the delay at Customs and a four-mile backup at the Harbor Tunnel, the expedition party didn't reach Sobotka's place on the southwestern shore of Bird River until dusk. As they puttered out Bird River on Sobotka's skiff, Chaplin set the scene: "The swamp whined with mosquitoes and through the trees will-o-the-wisps of sulfurous marsh gas bloomed like luminous flowers." Once docked at Stump's Swamp, the group trekked on foot for what seemed like hours, following Sobotka around stagnant pools and through tangles of lasso vines. "You get off this trail, it's like walking on thin ice," Sobotka warned. "You can feel the whole ground bending under you, you know, like a crust, some kind of permafrost. And caves and tunnels. The whole place is honeycombed."

It was 10:30 before the party finally set up camp in a low hummock of ground. A strong, new smell became evident the moment they arrived, one very different from the sulfurous marsh gas. Nobody knew the source of the smell, and they weren't sure they wanted to know.

Around the midnight hour, Chaplin was baiting a trap with chicken when he heard a loud *snap*. It was a "sharp, solid sound like a breaking bone." Whatever had made such a large branch break must have put a lot of weight on it.

"Did you hear that?" Chaplin whispered.

Ginny turned on the 650-watt spotlight and the forest was suddenly "as sharp, brilliant and cutting as broken glass." Swanson, his instincts quick from years as a war photographer, grabbed a camera from his pack. Looking through the viewfinder, Swanson panned the camera across the illuminated trees, trying to catch a shot of the monster.

Nothing. Whatever had been there a moment earlier had disappeared.

Helen's psychic sense was heightened by the excitement. "I know it now," she said. "This is the right place."

They turned off the spotlight and blew out the kerosene lanterns. Ginny set up the sound equipment, inserted a cassette, and played what was supposed to mimic the mating call of a Sasquatch. The sound was described as being "oddly nondirectional, like a siren, high-pitched falsetto." Helen said it sounded like music. Sobotka said it sounded like his ex-wife. Ten minutes later, the cassette clicked off. In the silence, like an echo, Helen thought she heard an answer.

Since White Marsh residents had said the creature seemed to like music, Chaplin and company decided to intersperse the Sasquatch calls with Jimmy Buffett. They cranked up the stereo and played "Mother, Mother Ocean," while the swamp crickets sang along.

At 4:30, the swamp began to lighten with a new day. While the rest of his party slept, Chaplin sat at the edge of the camp, staring off into the morning mist, pondering the likelihood of the Snallygaster:

> The fact is that too many honest and reliable people have seen these things. Too many newspapers have been publishing too many stories about them for too many years. The question is no longer: DID these people see anything? Rather, it is: WHAT did they see?

Although Chaplin's party had failed to gather any physical evidence that night, his attitude at the end of the report was one of clear-headed vigilance:

> We have the spirit and supplies to wait for months. We can put up with momentary setbacks and frustrations.

We have come into this with no stars in our eyes. We know the value of perseverance.

The editor's postscript was abrupt and chilling: *Chaplin's dispatch ends here. No further word at this printing has been received from the expedition.*

Chapter 5: Origin of the Snallygaster

Middletown Valley Register editor George C. Rhoderick and staff writer Ralph S. Wolfe are often attributed with popularizing the Snallygaster with a series of articles in 1909 and 1932. But did these two mischief-making journalists actually *invent* the beast, as several sources indicate? While no known written record of a winged, Western Maryland monster existed before 1909, there is evidence that the legend may have been part of the region's oral history almost one hundred and seventy-five years prior to the *Register* reports.

As documented in *History of Frederick County*, the first German settlers moved from Pennsylvania into the Old State Line as early as 1729. According to Alice T. Weinberg's *Spirits of Frederick*, the Snallygaster legend migrated to Middletown with German settlers in 1735. Furthermore, in the October, 1952 issue of *American Speech*, Leo Spitzer speculated that the name of the "legendary Maryland creature" must hark back to German folklore imported by the Pennsylvania Dutch[22]. The word *snallygaster* comes from *snollygoster*, which itself is a corruption of the German *schnelle geister*, meaning "quick spirits." According to *Haunted Maryland:*

---

[22] The Pennsylvania Dutch are German immigrants who settled in Pennsylvania beginning in 1689. In the English language of the 18th and 19th Centuries, the word "Dutch" referred to anyone from a wide range of Germanic regions, including areas that are now the Netherlands, Belgium, Germany, Austria, and Switzerland.

Ghosts and Strange Phenomena of the Old State Line, these spirits were said to have powers to "move things around or cause unexplained noises and unpleasant smells."

South Mountain Magic tells of schnelle geister that were seen on a "crisp and cold" Halloween night:

> The circlets of smoke took on a vaporous glamour, but yet defined it as opaque. Some moments later, numerous shrouded wraiths marshaled in mid-air on the brow of the declivity. Presently they ranked in approaching columns, with a swaying movement. A flash of intelligent apprehension seized both lookers-on, for now there was no mistaking the illusion of phantom hosts forming for conflict!

This spectral tale is clearly rooted in the ancient Germanic myth of the Wild Hunt: phantom hunters on horseback who storm through the air.

In his article, Spitzer explores the relationship between the Snallygaster and *wilde Jagd* (Wild Hunt):

> ...that is, from the troup of ghosts or damned souls believed to ride the air, with great noise of horses and hounds, between Christmas and Epiphany or on Hallowe'en under the guidance of the Wild Hunter (who is ultimately the Germanic weather god Woden), and to attempt to carry with them anybody they meet (especially children).

More evidence of the Snallygaster's child-snatching behavior originating with the Wild Hunt can be found in Kvelduf Hagen Gundarsson's essay, "The Folklore of the Wild Hunt and the Furious Host:"

> The motif of the living person who is picked up by the horde and carried somewhere else is particularly

common in Germany and in Norway...In Pomerania, doors are closed against the Hunter to keep children from being carried off; in Bohuslün, it was said that "Oden fares from up in the air and takes creatures and children with him.

The widely held belief that painting a seven-pointed star on one's barn is the best defense against the Snallygaster is rooted in the Dutch Pennsylvania folk art of hex signs. As defined by Don Yoder in his book *Hex Signs*, hex signs are "geometrical decorations in the form of large stars of various formats painted on the facades or gable ends of Pennsylvania barns." Although generations of Pennsylvania Dutch descendents have insisted that the unique decorations are "just for show," the theory that these signs were originally painted to ward off evil has floated around since the 1920s.

Wallace Nutting's *Pennsylvania Beautiful*, published in 1924, is credited with turning this mysterious but benign symbol into a "demonic lightning rod", as quoted by Yoder :

> The ornaments on barns found in Pennsylvania, and to some small extent West Jersey[23], go by the local name of hexafoos, or witch foot...They are supposed to be a continuance of very ancient tradition, according to what these decorative marks were potent to protect the barn, or more particularly the cattle, from the influence of witches.

After a 1929 witchcraft-related murder in York County, Pennsylvania became a media sensation and the word hex (German for witch) was added to the contemporary American lexicon. The demonic association with this once quaint, regional folk art was forever ingrained in our public consciousness.

---

[23] This author has seen hex signs painted on barns in Maryland, just south of Gettysburg.

Pennsylvania Dutch hex sign   *Photograph courtesy of Kevin Griffin Moreno*

While the most common motifs found on traditionally painted barns include four-, five-, six-, eight- and twelve-point stars, it was the alleged "seven-pointed star" that captured the imagination of the demon-fearing public. Although no seven-pointed has ever been known to exist in regional folk art, it has become an iconic image in the Pennsylvania Dutch mythology by way of tourist literature purveyors and sensationalist journalists. According to Ann Hark's *Hex Marks the Spot*, the hex signs that appeared in the "the magic number seven afforded full protection from acts of God and acts of witches both."

Leo Spitzer again references the ancient Wild Hunt when marrying the seven-pointed star to the Snallygaster:

> ...the folklorist will recognize in this description a variant of the belief in the 'seven whistlers' (Spenser: 'the Whistler shrill that who so hears doth die';

Wordsworth: 'the seven birds...that never part') who in turn are a popular derivation from the Wild Host...The 'hunt of Judas Maccebee' consists generally of seven members, which number explains both the 'seven whistlers' of Derbyshire and the seven-pointed star supposed to protect us against the snallygaster (i.e. against seven *schnelle Geister*).

South Mountain Magic is filled with tales of deadly snakes and basilisks that reportedly terrorized the region, but one in particular seems to evoke the Snallygaster:

An old woman told us that the snake mountaineers most dreaded was the hoop; but that this kind was so very rarely met with that, although she had lived in the woods all her life, she had never seen but one. If one-tenth the terrors with which her imagination invested this serpent are true, or indeed, if there is such a serpent at all, the presence of even one in the forest would be about as formidable as the fabled flying Dragon.

On one memorable occasion, the old woman was ascending the pinnacle of South Mountain with friends when they saw "something green spread out at length upon the sward. While they stood curiously looking at it, suddenly it put its tail in its mouth, raised its horn, and began to roll." The travelers swiftly climbed a rail fence when the thing rolled by, leaving a "slimy" track in its wake. The description of the beast recalls classic Germanic dragonlore:

This terrible serpent, as here described by an illiterate country woman, is but a repetition of the monsters that were said to spread such dismay and ruin that half the romances of knightly exploits were based upon the glory of their destruction.

While the Snallygaster/snollygoster/schnelle geister is not referenced by name in Dahlgren's collection of local legends, the monster's physical description (dragon-like) and behavior (child-snatching) were already entrenched in the local lore by 1876.

It would be another thirty-three years before the Snallygaster was pulled out of the shadows of obscure folklore and into the spotlight of the local media.

A century before *The Weekly World News* started running headlines like "Hilary Clinton Adopts Alien Baby," hoax journalism could be found in newspapers across the country, from small town weekly publications to big city dailies. From the end of the Civil War to the beginning of the 20th Century, United States newspaper readership rose from 10% to 26% of the adult population. This was the result of a sharp decline in the nation's illiteracy rate (20% to 10.7%) due to an increasing population and urbanization. Suddenly, newspapers were big business and publications found themselves printing outrageously fabricated stories to compete for readership in an increasingly crowded market.

Some of the more famous hoaxes were masterminded by our most celebrated authors, according to Lee Krystek, creator of the Web site, "Museum of Unnatural Mystery." Before becoming a national treasure, Mark Twain cut his journalistic teeth at a small Virginia City, Nevada paper, where he wrote a fake story about a man who "killed his wife and then went running through the streets of the town 'with his throat cut from ear to ear' while he carried his wife's still warm scalp with him." In 1844, the *New York Sun* published an account of a man who crossed the Atlantic in a balloon, one hundred years *before* the accomplishment actually occurred. The author of the balloon hoax? Edgar Allan Poe.

As America gave birth to the 20th Century, the public began to demand more accuracy from newspapers. Most major papers dropped their hoax stories as a new era of fact-checking and journalistic integrity emerged. But in an effort to boost dwindling circulation, the editorial staff of the *Middletown Valley Register* revived the hoax tradition, and created, quite literally, a monster.

Based on the striking similarities between the Snallygaster and Pennsylvania Dutch folklore, not to mention the beast's etymological origin, it is highly debatable whether two *Register* staff members— namely George C. Rhoderick, Sr. and Ralph S. Wolfe—actually *invented* the legend, as some have claimed. But even if the legend precedes the reporting of 1909, Rhoderick and Wolfe should be credited for popularizing the legend and attributing the monster with unique physical features. While certain characteristics—such as wings, tails, talons, and eggs—are obviously inspired by European dragonlore, the creature's more flamboyant descriptions (monocular vision and octopus tentacles) were most likely created to grab the reader's attention. "Journalists created hundreds of hoaxes about unusual animals, often monsters," writes Fred Fedler, in his essay "A Journalists' Favorite Hoax: Petrifications." "If journalists decided to write about a monster, for example, they tried to create a monster that was bigger, louder and more dangerous than any of the monsters described by their rivals."

In many respects, tracing the Snallygaster's newspaper history is just as difficult as tracing its folktale roots. Fedler expounds upon this point:

> When journalists create a hoax, no matter how preposterous, some readers will believe it. Moreover, other journalists will notice and reprint the story, not knowing (or perhaps caring) that the details are fictitious. For years after that, Americans browsing through old newspapers will find copies of it, and other media will reprint the copies. Thus, a good hoax may continue to appear and reappear for 50 or even 100 years. Unfortunately, it is difficult, often impossible, for historians to determine who created the hoax and which newspaper was first to publish it.

If the Snallygaster was indeed based on Pennsylvania Dutch folklore, what prompted the *Register* to resurrect it nearly 175 years later? The answer may lie to the north.

In January, 1909, only weeks before the Snallygaster story broke in Western Maryland, New Jersey papers reported their own giant, winged monster allegedly roaming the rural Pine Barrens region of the Garden State. As described by James F. McCloy and Ray Miller, Jr. in their regional classic *The Jersey Devil*, the creature had "the body of a kangaroo, the head of a dog, the face of a horse, the wings of a bat, the feet of a pig, and a forked tail."

Could the Snallygaster and the Jersey Devil—both referred to as "jabberwocks" by their respective newspapers—actually be the same monster? *The Jersey Devil* detailed a newspaper article that strongly echoed an earlier letter to the editor of the *Middletown Valley Register* concerning the "Department of Gyascutimoses."

> One tongue-in-cheek newspaper account was attributed to a Professor Breitkopf of the School of Science in Philidelphia. Breitkopf announced that the numerous tracks are made by prehistoric animals, obviously, peleosaurus cattellya of the Jurassic Period. These beasts had survived in limestone caves which had sunk beneath the Gulf Stream. With trapped air, fresh water and food, the life cycle continued.

The similarities don't end with volcanic activity and cave dwelling. Like the Snallygaster, the Jersey Devil phenomenon had apparently captured the interest of the Smithsonian Institution. And according to McCloy and Miller, the Jersey Devil "had not only been seen in south Jersey and eastern Pennsylvania, but reportedly has appeared as far south as Maryland." In turn, the first report of the Snallygaster in the *Middletown Valley Register* claimed that the Go-Devil came from Jersey: "The creature was first heard from in New Jersey about a month ago, when its tracks in the snow were observed."

Being that two winged creatures with similar backgrounds and characteristics were reported within weeks, it is highly unlikely that their stories are unrelated. Was the beast's trip from New Jersey to Maryland part of its natural migration south? Was it a case of Mid Atlantic mass hysteria? Fedler provides a possible explanation:

It was difficult, however, for journalists to create hoaxes about topics that were truly new. Newspapers published too many of the hoaxes, and journalists' experience—and imaginations—were limited. Thus, while creating a hoax, most journalists selected a familiar topic: a topic that they had already thought or read about.

Unlike the Snallygaster, whose origins are a bit murkier, the Jersey Devil, also known as the Leeds Devil, was already a well-established legend by the time the 1909 reports poured in. There is some evidence to suggest that Rhoderick and Wolfe were inspired by the New Jersey Devil phenomenon of 1909 to generate interest in their own local myth.

The link between these two monsters may go back even further. As legend has it, the Jersey Devil was the 13th child born to "Mother Leeds," an early matron in New Jersey folklore. The year of the birth? 1735: The same year the Snallygaster allegedly migrated to Middletown.

Chapter 6: Sign of the Times

While most hoaxes were published to entertain readers and boost circulation, sometimes the newspaper publishers created headlines to make a political or social point. The Snallygaster's emergence in 1909 and 1932 reflected two issues that were significant in the Progressive Era[24] South: African American segregation and the prohibition of alcohol.

Throughout its history, the Snallygaster has had a strong and often controversial association with the African American community. In the book *Weird and Wonderful Words*, Erin McKean refers to the Snallygaster as a "mythical monster of Maryland invented to frighten freed slaves." *Maryland: A Guide to the Old State Line*, the Federal Writers' Project[25] book published in 1940, describes the creature as a "fabulous reptilian bird of vast size that preys on poultry and Negro children after nightfall." This theme can be traced back to the *Middletown Valley Register*'s first Snallygaster story in 1909: "This vampire-devil only attacks colored people…It is

---

[24] During the period known as the Progressive Era (1890s to about 1920) the U.S. government became increasingly activist in both domestic and foreign policy. Reform-minded political leaders moved to extend their vision of a just and rational order to all areas of society.

[25] Established in 1935 by President Franklin Delano Roosevelt, the Federal Writers' Project (FWP) was established to fund written work and support writers during the Depression.

seldom seen during the day, feeding at night only, and the strange part is that is seems to prefer colored men to colored women, though it attacks the latter at times."

The following quote from the February 19, 1909, edition of the *Register* suggests that the Snallygaster stories may have been politically motivated:

> Emanuel Myers, a well known colored man of Middletown, says that the report of a go-devil being seen in the valley don't bother him a bit. He says the only devil he is worried about is the Democratic amendment next fall.

The amendment in question was certainly the Straus Amendment, a Democratic proposal that intended to restrict the voting rights of African Americans. Could the Snallygaster have been a metaphor for the state Democrats, a political party the Republican newspaper viewed as trying to disenfranchise blacks? Consider the *American Heritage Dictionary* definition of *snollygoster*: "One, especially a politician, who is guided by personal advantage rather than by consistent, respectable principles. Perhaps alteration of *snallygaster*, a mythical beast said to prey on poultry and children." Interestingly enough, on February 12, 1909, the very same day the first Snallygaster appeared in the *Middletown Valley Register*, the National Association for the Advancement of Colored People (NAACP) was founded.

Regardless of whether the *Register* ran the Snallygaster stories to make a political point or merely to scare blacks, not all readers were amused. Reader R. Austin articulated his distaste in a letter to the editor:

> ...whatever the purpose of this item, whether it is intended to be funny, to scare a certain class of people for some hidden reason, or for any other purpose, it seems to me to be of questionable merit...anything that may have the affect of creating fear in the heart of any

man, be he white or black, in my humble opinion should be condemned.

During the 1932 Democratic National Convention, presidential nominee Franklin D. Roosevelt all but declared war on Prohibition, pledging to "favor the modification of the Volstead Act[26] just as fast as the Lord will let us authorize the manufacture and sale of beer." In contrast, the *Middletown Valley Register* strongly favored upholding the dry law, calling Prohibition the "greatest issue since the days of slavery."

Ten days after Roosevelt won the Presidency by a landslide, the *Register* announced the reemergence of the Snallygaster:

> Some persons who saw the monster, which is being described as large as a dirigible, believe that it is an omen of evil as a result of the recent election…One man who claims to have seen the monster a few days ago, stated to "The Register" representative that he had believed the beast was an omen of ill for colored voters who deserted the Republican party in the Presidential election and voted for Roosevelt. Of course, it is needless to say that this man was an ardent Hoover supporter.

After Roosevelt was elected President on November 8, the *Register* feared that a repeal of the 18th Amendment wasn't far behind. In a subversive display of support for Prohibition, the newspaper boiled the Snallygaster in a vat of illegal moonshine and triumphantly announced its death: "The action of two prohibition agents will certainly be welcome news to persons residing in the various sections where the beast was seen, for they can now lay down their arms and once more enjoy a quiet night's rest."

---

[26] The Volstead Act, named after Chairman of the House Judiciary Committee Andrew Volstead, reinforced the prohibition of alcohol in the United States.

Much to the *Register*'s chagrin, on March 23, 1933, President Roosevelt signed into law an amendment to the Volstead Act known as the Cullen–Harrison Act, allowing the manufacture and sale of certain kinds of alcohol. The 18th Amendment was repealed with ratification of the 21st Amendment, on December 5, 1933.

Epilogue

Over the past 273 years, the Snallygaster has evolved from a fast moving ghost, to a winged, one-eyed, go-devil, to a big and hairy dwayyo. It's been a trickster. A predator. A harbinger of evil. It's been a myth. A hoax. A Psychic Sasquatch from Outer Space. It's been hunted. Killed. Manipulated for political gain. It has been reportedly seen from the Eastern Panhandle of West Virginia to Maryland's Eastern Shore, and everywhere in between, as well as making appearances as far away as Ohio and New Jersey.

By the 1980s, the Snallygaster had become little more than a curiosity for local historians. A brief *Frederick News Post* piece entitled "A Snallygaster Story" that ran on the tenth page of the September 7, 1983 edition was a charming summary of the local legend. For older residents, the story was a nostalgic re-acquaintance with an old tale. For newcomers and those too young to remember, the story served as an interesting tidbit of local trivia.

The Snallygaster has all but been forgotten in the 21st Century. Older residents have died or moved away, and their memories of growing up with the Snallygaster have gone with them. And as farmland is replaced with shopping centers and woods are cleared for housing developments, so go the legend's haunts.

Although the mark of the beast has faded with time, remnants continue to remind us of its legacy. There's the Snallygaster gift shop that sells fine handcrafted gifts and jewelry in downtown Middletown; its business cards emblazed with a sketch of the creature. The children's menu of favorite Frederick eatery Barley & Hops also adorns a rendering of the dreaded Snallygaster. In August 2007, 1980s local indie rockers The Skeptics reunited for one last show at the Frederick Cultural Arts Center. On stage in front of an enthusiastic crowd, the hard-rocking trio blazed through songs from their one LP, *Snallygaster*. The album art, which features a razor-beaked, one-eyed Snallygaster, was illustrated by Skeptics drummer and Frederick native, Stephen Blickenstaff.

The Snallygaster has even, in a few instances, transcended regional interest and infiltrated popular culture nationwide. The cartoon family the Flintstones encountered the beast in the 1972 childrens' book, *Fred Flintstone and the Snallygaster*. Snallygaster was also the name of a beverage composed of Mountain Dew and vanilla ice cream, created by Mountain Dew in the 1960s to promote the soft drink.

Whether the Snallygaster is an ancient folk legend, a hoax created by politically motivated newspaper editors, or a little bit of both, the monster is now an indelible part of our local history. Throughout its history, the legend has been exploited, dismissed, explained and even killed. But it refuses to stay away for long. It lies waiting. In the caves of South Mountain. In our collective imagination. In our memories and the histories of our ancestors.

On that dark night in Stump's Swamp, Helen Chaplin told her husband that she thought the beast would appear because they believed in it.

I agree.

As long as we keep the campfire story alive, the Snallygaster will be with us. But the fire is dying. It's up to us to tell the tale.

Bibliography

Books

Bloecher, Ted. *Report on the UFO Wave of 1947*. 1967.

Bord, Colin and Bord, Janet. *The Bigfoot Casebook*. Mechanicsburg, PA: Stackpole Books, 1982.

Cannon, Timothy L. and Whitmore, Nancy F. *Ghosts and Legends of Frederick County*. Frederick, MD: 1979.

Hark, Ann. *Hex Marks the Spot*. Philadelphia, PA: J.B. Lippincott Company, 1938.

McCloy, James F. and Miller Jr., Ray. *The Jersey Devil*. Wilmington, DE: The Middle Atlantic Press, 1976.

McKean, Erin. *Weird and Wonderful Words*. New York, NY: Oxford University Press, 2003.

Okonowicz, Ed. *Haunted Maryland: Ghosts and Strange Phenomena of the Old State Line*. Mechanicsburg, PA: Stackpole Books, 2007.

Vinton Dahlgren, Madeleine. *South Mountain Magic: Tales of Old Maryland*. Maple Shade, NJ: Lethe Press, 2002.

Weinberg, Alyce T. *Spirits of Frederick*. Frederick, MD: Studio 20, 1979.

Williams, T.J.C. *History of Frederick County Maryland Volume 1*. Frederick, MD: L. R. Titsworth & Co., 1910.

Writer's Program of the Work Projects Administration. *Maryland: a Guide to the Old State Line*. New York, NY: Oxford University Press, 1940.

Yoder, Don and Graves, Thomas E. *Hex Signs*. Mechanicsburg, PA: Stackpole Books, 2000.

Newspapers and Periodicals

"The Colored People are in Great Danger." Middletown Valley Register. 12, Feb. 1909.

"Emmitsburg Saw the Great Snallygaster." Middletown Valley Register. 5, Mar. 1909.

"Origin of the Great Snallygaster." Middletown Valley Register. 30, Jul. 1909.

"Strange Monster Mystifies and Alarms Persons Living in South Mountain Section." Middletown Valley Register. 18, Nov. 1932.

"2 Middletown Men See 'Snallygaster' Tuesday Morning." Middletown Valley Register 25, Nov. 1932.

Stine, Austin R. "Doesn't Like Snallygaster." Middletown Valley Register. Letter. 25, Nov. 1932.

Jones, Mrs. Lewis E. "This Reader Enjoys the Snallygaster Stories." Letter. Middletown Valley Register. 2, Dec. 1932.

"Bovalopus Obliterated By the Same Hand Which Brought Huge Monster Into Existence." Middletown Valley Register. 2, Dec. 1932.

"Snallygaster Story Spreads." Frederick Post. 1, Dec. 1932.

"Snallygaster Story Goes On the Air Monday." The Frederick News. 13, Dec. 1932.

"Snallygaster Story is Revived at Middletown." Frederick News. 23, Jul. 1934.

"Five Jet Planes Sped Over Frederick in Late Afternoon." Frederick News. 8, Jul. 1947.

"Snallygaster Talk Back in Middletown." Frederick News. 8, Jul. 1947.

May, George. "You'd Better Watch Out: 'Dwayyo' Could Be a Modern Snallygaster." Frederick News Post. 3, Mar. 1965.

"A Snallygaster Story." Frederick News Post. 7, Sept. 1983.

"New York Firemen Stayed the Flames." The New York Times. 9, Feb. 1904.

"Those Tracks – Bear or Just Imagination." The Washington Post. 12, Jul. 1952.

"Gorilla-Like Beast Seen Roaming Woods Near Elkton – In Md.'s 'Snallygaster Country." The Washington Post. 28, Aug. 1953.

Chaplin, Gordon. "The Grand Bicentennial Washington Post/Potomac Expedition to Darkest Maryland in Search of the Monstrous Snallygaster." The Washington Post. 10, Oct. 1976.

Gundarsson, Kveldulf Hagen. "The Folklore of the Wild Hunt and the Furious Host." Mountain Thunder. Issue 7, Winter 1992.

Smith, Van. "Q and A With John Lutz." Baltimore City Paper. 23, Mar. 2005

Spitzer, Leo. "Snallygaster." American Speech. Vol. 27, No. 3. Oct., 1952.

Web

Krystek, Lee. "Hoax Journalism." The Museum of Unnatural Mystery. http://www.unmuseum.org

Fedler, Fred. "A Journalists' Favorite Hoax: Petrifications." Historybuff.com. http://www.historybuff.com/library/refpetrification.html

About the Author

Patrick Boyton is a writer and filmmaker with an MFA from New York University. He lives in Frederick, MD with his wife Melissa, in-laws Rich and Rose, and their pug, Lilly. Patrick's interests include movies, folklore and local history.

About the Illustrator

R. M. Hanson is an Illustrator / Designer / Fine Artist with a BFA from the Minneapolis College of Art and Design. He enjoys monsters, ghosts, horror movies, bicycles, and sushi. You can find more of his artwork and design at http://www.rmhanson.com.